NIGHT JOURNEY

Also by Josephine Dickinson

Scarberry Hill
The Voice
Silence Fell

NIGHT JOURNEY

Josephine Dickinson

For Patricia Reed

With best wishes

Josephine Dickinson

FlambardPress

First published in Great Britain in 2008 by Flambard Press
Stable Cottage, East Fourstones, Hexham NE47 5DX
www.flambardpress.co.uk

Typeset by BookType
Cover Design by Gainford Design Associates
Printed in Great Britain by Cromwell Press, Trowbridge, Wiltshire

A CIP catalogue record for this book is available from the British Library.
ISBN: 978-1-906601-01-0

Flambard Press wishes to thank Arts Council England for its financial support.

Flambard Press is a member of Inpress

Acknowledgements

Several poems previously appeared in the following journals and magazines: 'Night Journey' in *Dream Catcher*; 'The Story of the Two Kegs', 'Silly Hall', 'Darkness' and 'The Butterfly' in *The Rialto*; 'This Night' in *Gilsland Village Magazine*; 'The Three Bearing Gifts' and 'The Birth' in *PNR*; 'You' and 'In the Darkness' in *Ploughshares*.

'Spells of the Raven' was commissioned for *Cumbria Life* magazine by East Cumbria Countryside Project, and appears in the anthology *An Accessible Paradise*, edited by Dick Capel.

'Mass' (from the sequence 'This Night') appears in the Seren anthology *Women's Work* (2008) edited by Amy Wack.

The passage by Galway Kinnell on the cover is from his Foreword to the author's US volume *Silence Fell* (2007), and is used by kind permission of Houghton Mifflin.

The cover image is from an oil pastel, 'Night Journey', by Lorna Graves (1947–2006), and is used by kind permission of the Lorna Graves trustees Judith Clark and Jan Ellis. Thanks to Jeremy Latimer of the Lowood Gallery who made this possible.

The author photograph is by John Hedgecoe, used by his kind permission and that of the Minneapolis *Star Tribune*, and with thanks to Sarah Williams.

'An Offering' was inspired by Bill Reid's bronze sculpture, 'The Spirit of Haida Gwaii, The Jade Canoe'. 'Never' draws on Éric Valli's book *Himalaya*. The final line of 'Fucking Venus' quotes the third line of Pindar's '1st Pythian Ode' as in Robert Duncan's 'A Poem Beginning With a Line From Pindar'. The title 'Hazy All Over Titan' was taken from a *Spaceflight Now* online bulletin. 'Interior Life' quotes and adapts passages from the *Electronic Text Corpus of Sumerian Literature*. 'Spells of the Raven' makes use of texts from the Gospel of Thomas, Robert Graves' *The White Goddess* and the Book of Job.

This collection could not have come to be without the generous and various help, encouragement and support of the following: staff and friends of Alston Cottage Hospital, Michael and Hetty Baron, Alice Bondi, Dick Capel, Ann Chesters, Michael Collier, Pat and Tim Cooke, Sally Dalglish, Caroline Dawnay, John Dixon, The Reverend Mary Dow, Emily Drake, Jim Edley, Afifa Ematullah, Jim Eynen, Hilary Fell, Alan Franks, Frances Gapper, Patricia Gorton, Stephen Gorton, Robert Green, Charlie Gurrey, Kathy Habberjam, Edie Harbord, Sue Harper, Katie-Ellen Hazeldene, John and

Jenny Hedgecoe, Henderson's Garage Alston, Joan Hewitt, Will Higgs, Matthew Hollis, Katie Hornby, Roger Hutchinson, Mike and Peter Jackson, Gillian Kay, Galway and Bobbie Kinnell, Roger and Ann-Marie Knight, Howard Laing, Margaret and Peter Lewis, Will Mackie, Michael Mackmin, Jenny Macmillan, Tanya Marsden, Moredun Garage Alston, Oona O'Beirn, Marita and Jeremy Over, Dean Parkin, Meg Peacocke, Connie Pickard, Tom Pickard, Nick Sawyer, Michael Schmidt, Elizabeth Stott, Paul Sutherland, Tommy Tarn, Jo Varney, Elizabeth Vegh, Angela Watson-Brown, Margaret and Peter Whyte, Sally Williams, Monsignor Peter Wilson, The Wordsworth Trust.

Contents

' . . . and when I shall die
Take him and cut him out in little stars,
And he will make the face of heaven so fine
That all the world will be in love with night
And pay no worship to the garish sun.'

Shakespeare, *Romeo and Juliet*

'It may be, that there is no such thing as an equable motion, whereby time may be accurately measured.'

Isaac Newton, *Principia, Scholium to Definition VIII*

A History of Moths

What were you thinking as you wintered the books?
Moth dark with soot they'd print your fingers black –
fingers that weighed them one by one and stacked
them, loosely classified, on sugared shelves
they'd carved themselves. Did you count them? Curse them? Or love
the chrysalidian spines, the nibbled leaves
grazed quickly on the wing from predators?
The crude handwritten bookmarks? Or was it more
the pupal bullion that no-one before
had touched you wanted to hatch as currency
to use, exchange, compare, admire? And me
you wanted to coin more books. A 'History
of Moths', perhaps? – A trove of fairy tales?
With endings next to which this other one pales?

An Offering

1. One Thing

The boat stinks of tar and purrs like a bull.
The air is still.
At prow and helm lit torches dribble.
Below nine people jostle
awkwardly: Bear, Beaver, Raven,
Mouse, Fish and Scorpion,
Frog, Wolf and Killer Whale.
Their exhalations grime the portholes.
Pots of flowers hum
with colour, flowers whose cultivation
has barely been attended through nine seasons:
the air alone has nourished their seed
(– otherwise wouldn't the boat have been alien,
unable to aspire to the one thing left unsaid?).

2. Mercy, Mercy, Mercy

A solitary whistle thrills the table,
a coruscating heckle.
Just this once Wolf holds his breath.
Raven stands, *lex talionis*
against mutiny.
Wheat and chaff in the septal alembic
shake, the spit and swallow mute the storm,
death is positioned as oppositional and tears and kisses fox the bird.

A moment's grace – then a copper chorus jars the crop hush,
the sea centres in the vein blood,
yields aching heart to syzygy.
New seed falls, light accrues in attar.
Raven accepts impotence – the harmony of the planet's secret eclipse
and oscillation of extremes in his breast centred in the air as the sea shifts.

3. A Reprieve

After a long time a bay arborescence dips
to their unison breathing, swish of tails, tread of easting heels.
As traces in the water clear to lucid,
they wriggle like puppets single file,
eyes discerning the flag and the crown,
the colour of the sky,
the air and water mixed, the mud,
their inheritance, the almagest, the bliss of inner cockles,
the wings that soar despite soreness of tendons.

The tree pursues silence. Breathing hard,
they stop on its dry leaf-crumple, reel
under the spell of the galley,
enthrone Wolf's double, dock his tongue's tip,
buck the merchant, tag on straws.

4. An Offering

There are flowers everywhere.
The passengers no longer imitate each other,
or attempt to steal land identities,
are happy to be on the boat, happy
to take relaxed steps together
on sea legs, being as they are,
shout at each other, back and forth,
tug tablecloths.
They lock Raven in his pulpit for the time being.
They'll review this at the first port of call.
Beaver, overwhelmed by the sound of water,
dreams on deck with Frog.
Killer Whale keeps her head down.
Scorpion alone is sceptical.
And Fish is aware of multitudes under the boards.

5. A Response

There is a soft tread somewhere of someone heavy,

> *(Mouse and Bear are equally soft),*

and in turmoil.

> *(They want to fight but they instead exchange their hearts.)*

He is home-sick.

> *(They know what it's like to be there
> even though they're not.)*

He is hidden.

> *(None can dissent.)*

He alone is consistent.

> *(Not afraid to know nothing, half of which
> is a name.)*

In a group he is a sleuth, so what is he alone?

> *(Nothing.)*

Mouse.

> *(Alone he has at least the gall to count.)*

Purse

Night and day I fester in the dark.
My pod is drained and squeezed in a crack,
crushed in a sink hole by the grike of a clint.
Mint sauce dribbles through cracks and joints.
My skin is oily. I am red and green.
I am lady threadneedle,
plump to the touch.

I shrug water off my back,
gushes vanish in my grot.
Take care not to tear
when you plumb the overflow.
My guts swell in the heat,
my inner pockets slip and slide,
my grommets are green slime.

You were picking a bone,
snapping me open and shut,
stuffing me with metal tongues,
cramming me with sycamore keys.
The Zeitgeist does not favour these.
But I hang on to them,
they prepare to stir.

Water slobbers over me like a laugh,
sluices crevices,
deluges my cavern.
One day my prize will grow,
my store proliferate.
I know that water never touches bottom
of the overflow.

If I Had Been Able to Show You Myself

But I couldn't, for in the light I be invisible.
You have a whole ocean, an ocean full
of me. I rise to the surface, glowing,
humped and quivering, holding

one note, reaching the next,
and floating, gulping, dip my canal,
shrug my bell, glug the salt
and sperm, in my own little sun,

from my hood to my rhopalium
feel the shocks of pain
run over me, into me, out of me,
pulse towards the light,

distended, clinch what is near,
relish the taste
and mystery caught in my net.
One mouth to eat, and one to shit,

four arms to dibble.
I be a circle, I be a womb in a sac,
I be Medusa without her head.
I suck the pits,

spadefish, sunfish, loggerheads me.
A touch trigger barbed coils,
sunk in my arms and tentacles.
Hundreds, thousands

stud my body.
It's not a thing I do.
You touch me.
It sting you.

Led By Three Clerks of the Highest Form

1

In Vlissingen the land is flat, all
is straight lines. A cemetery,
a geometrical garden. A field ploughed
all the way down. A solitary hedge
enclosing allotments and glass tunnel. A house,
white plaster garlands hung up along.
Tall narrow trees. Horizontal white slabs.
Large kidney-shaped pond. House
stubbled (yellow). Leafy alleyways.
Trees washed over in pollarded rows.
A sky of matt glass illuminated from behind.
Next to it a tennis court the same.

2

The choir is allowed to sit during the Epistle and Gradual.
The invisible sheet speckled with birds folds and unfolds.
While it is being sung three clerks of the highest
form don silken copes in the lizard-yellow
four turreted church, the twin black death-tower,
in the vestry, and go through the middle of the quire
into the rood loft, ready to begin the Alleluia.
Set in the slope a plain stone crucifix.
(Rock reddens.) A madonna stands in the corner
of a whitewashed house. Hoofprinted plaster. Bells.
After the Gradual the three second-formers bow
to the altar and return to their places,
terraces cut in the rock,
the rock with a yellow crown.

And the three seniors begin
the Alleluia. Lead rolls out like parchment over
curving buttresses. *Alleluia. Alleluia. Pascha*
nostrum immolatus est Christus. Alleluia.
Pinned to the breast of a hill a sculpted angel.
Alleluia. Epulemur in azymis
sinceritatis et veritatis. Alleluia.
River breaks in waves. We see
sun's light on river through a colonnade.
Alleluia.

3

A blind mother holds her baby's head,
like a grey pebble pulsing in and out
of visibility in a dark space
under high turrets.
A barn collapses to its knees. It moves.
Even here I feel it. Splitting of struts.
Under an arch a procession of monks. A tree flops
apart. Elsewhere, a dead mother
entombs her own raw baby. I live.

4

The turrets leap in and out of visibility.
Where can I find some water?
Best is water. And gold. Brightest is sun,
this music. But they lie.
Inspection of the roof space showed deflection
of purlins and some splitting of struts.
This is not a language. The world exploded –
it moves space. A woman crouched, half cat,
over there. Grace gives truth to falsehood.
At birdsmouths rooftiles had been laid
directly onto battens. And when the debris cleared
I found myself in an enormous monastery,
half (woman) human. The highlighted tree
sparks the storm air.
Where can I find some water?

5

The Lorelei looks like charred wood. All
these castles make a point of having holes.
How come an entire hill is a different colour?
Because of an accident of seed.
In the patch where the turnips are ready to break
out of the soil, here live your life
out! Burn it! A square of blue high up
among the yellow. Towers and turrets
let sun through, sunset and dawn.
A little white house like a hat. Meccano set
railway over the river. Gold-tipped cupola.
A bicycle leans against the house. They assemble.
On the delicate skin of water let
an infinite alternation of black and white.
The holes show different colours
at different times of day and night.

Night Journey

In this yew,
silver-lipped bole,
divine the true
age of the year.
Whatever your wish,
to be still,
to tremble,
is hallowed here.

My bark is hollowed.
The wound
has revealed
the age of the moon
by her reflection
in my silver womb.

Hold me,
sea,
that I would be
a craft that sets
sail in calm
or storm,
by day, stars
or planets.

Who but you to provide
the state of the tide?
A boat without guide
needs only sea.
Unafraid to drown,
or to land alone
on sand at dawn,
hull empty.

The Story of the Two Kegs

This is my second run of luck.
The first was when earth caught
me neatly like a ball from three flights up –
and now keg-lifting in the basement with friends.
I must indeed have been born
with a silver spoon in my mouth.
Why was it the sounds I longed for most?
After the terrible noise, collapse
of walls, silence. I tried my best
with folksongs, stories, but silence was like
a seventh prisoner, trapped with us.
It was thirty-five days, they say.
We never doubted we would be rescued.
It was outside time, I now know –
the darker side of time. The cold
was like a hammer. My bed, some sacking
between two kegs, felt like a knife.
Sleep was a pause in electric shock.
I got used to the taste of pickles
on my breath, bottled fruit and vegetables,
exquisite shaved slices of ham.
It was black as the inside of a pitched keg.
We had a few matches: every time
we struck one (the walls of the basement bucked
like a bull) we were shocked how small it was.
The smell, of course, got worse and worse,
but it was the smell of life, not death –
though at any time it could have changed.
Do you know the story of the two kegs?
Let me sing it to you before you go mad.
The knocking (we screamed out), scraping, dragging,
everything different, gone, a white hole.

The Dark Tower

He had found my notebook, my miracle of technology, in a carrier bag,
with rotten tomatoes, frying pan scrapings and carpet underlay. Could
he speak to me about it? Of course, I said. Let's meet in the Gogol Bar
where there's shadow enough to see you by. He came, en route for home,
off duty. Sat and chatted. Asked if I'd like a gin? Said no. He insisted. Got
one each, both filled to the brim. It was a crumbling, chunky thing,
black covers, red corners, red spine, the black worn off of the edges,
flecked and dented, full of a tiny hand in various coloured
inks, both right way up and upside down, John Cage's
hand *The White House 1pm*, some random jottings,
sketches, stories, bits of blotting paper, a letter
requesting South Bank comps, conversations on photography,
Chopin, Derrida, sex, Artaud. He started. How it happened,
hordes of androgynous women stood at a turnstile I was passing through
and for some strange reason a bull with massive horns was tethered
there. I stood for a moment, mesmerised by the syrupy sheen
of the animal's hide as it flexed and twisted. In another moment the beast
had snapped his tether, dipped his horns and, snatching a woman,
smashed her down on the concrete three or four times. The shadows
in the Gogol Bar were rich and dark as he spoke from under
his broad felt brim. A little bar tucked in the top of Serendip
Street behind a plane tree. No street tables. All the seats
downstairs in a row of snugs with a single shaded lamp
on each table, benches either side. No windows. Matt
mahogany surfaces. Standing smoke. He continued. Where
I found your book was a tower in a hidden, fenced-off field, with a steam-
flanked snow-white stallion stamping in the mist. I followed
a winding woodland path behind a lake, past an upturned
rowboat, reeds as tall as elephants, hovering haze,
on a moonlit night. The tower had a hollow wall with indentations,
a flaking roof, a gravel floor, an upstairs window.
There, in the ghastly light of the moon stood a willowy figure,
hands outheld, with a glassy stare, percipient
or not, or indeed whether live or dead, was hard to tell.
I ducked inside. A table was there, and on it the bag, the smelly jumble
spilling out of it. And, at the bottom, your book, and in the book
these very scenes I'm telling, on a page you'd marked *Delphinium Formosum*.

The Dress

A stranger had come to visit and I handed back to him a heavy,
twice folded bundle. He accepted it solemnly, gave a little bow,
retreated. He had laid the dress on my bed, its black panels spread to show
the rich encrustations of embroidered crimson rectangles, repeated
geometrical patterns made up of agglomerations of jewel
coloured cross stitches, which appeared to be trees as crystals, partial accounts
of twigs and rivers and landscapes, gorgeous fields of amber, blue and green, down
to the hem, with golden shimmer placed to catch the light in a specific
direction, so that from each angle the patterns were new, and turquoise knotted
bands twisted round the bib and the elbows and down the arms, and zigzags of
black cotton showed underneath where the blocks of stitching had been applied,
and the front skirt billowed to contain pregnancy for which generations of
women would have worn it and married in it and they carried babies in it,
patched it, laundered it with perfumed water, felt the cool breeze enter the deep
and narrow scoop at the front, where rested also a string of amber beads
with a burn mark near the clasp at the nape of the neck. I had taken off
all my clothes to put on this embroidered dress. The weight of all the stitches
added to it one at a time, each one at a specific moment in
her life by a specific woman in Palestine, its purchase twenty years
ago in Israel for a huge sum, and the knowledge that I was the first
to wear the dress since then seemed sufficient as the fields burned into my skin.

Tracking Venus

1. Never

Here, in the mountains, near where the river narrows,
flows faster, and rocks tumbled in a ring enclose
pools of still water, the dead are buried, their tools
at their head, and tigers roam, and clear water drifts
over the rocks carrying the foam of Never,
barely moving over the stones of the river-
bed, slowly, tenderly. Never has a secret
lover, No-One, who likes to hunt in the lonely
forest with his twin brother. They are wanderers.
Rather than fight for their territory, gods, way
of life, they prefer to exist, deep in the heart
of the forest. For myself I have never met
them. They are alone with nature. They collect herbs
in the woods, use their magic to gather nectar.
They are said to have the power to protect a land
from tigers. Knowledge, watchfulness are their only
weapons against evil. In the flowing silver,
at one particularly tumultuous spot,
the water, passing over a stone shelf, is squeezed
and brought bubbling up from Hell through a narrow gap.
It's the Devil. In the centre of the outflow,
its edges slowly rotating anticlockwise,
is a slick of pale blue light on the sucking,
licking surface of the water as barbed, spiked flakes
fall. The Devil wants his daughter, Never, married.
Marriage in the forest is the exchange of bread
and mutual benedictions on the forehead.
Magic is used to entice our daughters, transform
them into members of their species. But he wants
Never married to the King in a church in Hell.
And a man in the village has claimed Never as
his. Someone the Devil detests. If No-One dies

his bow and arrows will be left in the forest
at his head, just as his mother's pots full of rice
were left at hers, before the forest people left
that site, never to return. But Never has her
father's barbed magic whip, blue-white incandescence
in the west. With it she is able to perform
magic. As for the forest people, those silent men,
of whom she loves No-One, they avoid villagers.
They travel in small groups led by The One Who Walks
Ahead. They carry light gear and food in baskets.
They pitch camp in an afternoon, huts of branches
covered with leaves, too low to stand but wide enough
for a small family to curl up in at night
against the cold and damp. Never's arranged marriage
is soon. The Devil hates the man. The Devil said
to the King: 'You'll see what happens when you enact
your new law. Never's in danger of bewitchment
by a wild lover from the forest. But I shall
watch her – above the wall, through the wall, through holes my
blue light penetrates.' He's set her impossible
tasks, which I, as village crier, had to announce.
To make a meadow of a lake and cut the hay
as snowflakes fly. To make a vineyard of a wood
and gather grapes for the wine in an icy wind.
To find the low bridge which descends onto a high.
To build a real church with a cross of ice in Hell.
What she doesn't know is what the Devil wants it
for – her wedding to the King. She's done the first three,
cut rushes, made wild berry wine and found Natrass,
but can't do the last. I've been told to beat the drums
and announce that from this day villagers must give
the King a quarter of all beer brewed in each house
and the choicest parts of any pig that is killed.
Also, wives must spend the night before their marriage
with the King at the palace. Never will be like
Daphne fleeing Apollo. She will try to do
her magic against it. As the Leaping Ferret

stream grows in dark places, trembles in its narrow
pebbly furrow. With crackles, slurps, under the ice
sheets it shatters against the Devil. It won't melt,
rattles uselessly. Even though women who drink
the water of the snows of the mountains fallen
from the rocks which bear the essence of the Lizard
King have an essence of fire. The ripples back up
against the flow, the stream is frozen. She can't do
her magic, even with her father's whip, frozen
in ribbled sheets, knubbles, marbles, spikes and knuckles,
sticks of ice cobbled together to beat his wife.

2. Knowing When Love Is Real (or Psyche's Dream)

In Paradise
is the treasure in the field,
two birds in a tree,
a child, a simple child,
a duck in a pond.
And Psyche,
walking out at dusk,
sees a blonde,
and recognises,
pushing a pram, the mother of Eros
with her young son.

Psyche,
pushed on the razor's edge
by her two sisters,
dodges behind a tree
and on
to the top of the hill
and back, and sees
what she fears.
Eros? –
a cat with golden wings, intense and sexed –
or his double?

Paradise in the dark.
Lightning.
Two golden birds
which sing
in an alder tree.
A dragon in a hole.
Psyche puts nothing in.
The dragon eats it all,
spits out a skeleton,
turns into a deep-fleeced, conch-horned ram,
and disappears.

3. Son of the Ban-Sidhe

Blue sky came to earth,
with music and all the tongues,

to Psyche in her cage,
under cover of night.

He forbade her look at his face
(the power of him!) or speak.

She must not look.
She must not speak.

Awakes as one but more than one,
she on his left, he on her right,

whose being is one,
both parting and reunion,

image, light and eye,
boy on dolphin's back.

But she does look and speaks.
A door opens, a secret place.

She quakes to see the Ban-Sidhe,
woman of faery race,

her blinding light. Looks,
and is transfixed.

This is she herself speaking.
She overpowered herself,

burnt him as he lay asleep,
with the intelligence in the breast.

He awoke and vanished,
and all the intelligence lost.

It was inevitable –
he who was, before his mother.

And so she works in the dark,
attempts the impossible.

I falter before this task, I falter,
to find words as sky finds earth,

to adequately express
the incalculable –

as he sees her as she is –
paradox, and consciousness.

Though I speak with tongues of men
and of angels and have not love . . .

love bears all things,
endures, speaks . . .

Earth moves towards day.
Tears roll down his cheeks.

She clings to his foot.
She goes to hell

and back.
But, keeps the beauty.

4. Tracking Venus

In June you brushed with the Sun.
And now Sun's metal fruit meets Titan, Saturn's moon,
a parachute moment,
a ripe fruit

dropped in a frozen
tangerine sky, bang
in enchantment
of gravity,

for brief
awakening on the moon,
a meeting
of you and the Sun.

As you mingle your spume,
dissolving deep in each other's eyes,
crawl over each other's bodies, spreading
clamours of birds

in an acre of northern forest
at dawn, cling tight,
entwine your legs, every
spot of his body

burns and fingertips prickle,
he winks and resonates
the 80,000 years your golden sandals
take to appear

(they are light in darkness, darkness in light),
alight for the journey.
The strobe of the heat
and the blue

that pulses between you is audible. Then,
'Before you go,' he says, as you moan and begin to move apart,
'I need to show you
one or two things:

how the dolphin is sacred to Neptune and Apollo,
the grass and the blooms that grow
in the tracks of your beautiful feet, and the tempests
of Titan.'

5. *Fucking Venus*

Pythagoras reveres The Self, The Godhead. Venus is the only planet bright
enough. On this question there is cast a shadow. Venus is the closest silence
within me. She is 108 million kilometres from the Sun and has a 243-day rotation period.
And she has no moon. Earth is 150 million kilometres from the Sun. Venus is a similar
size to Earth, 12,100 kilometres diameter. Always close to the Sun as seen from Earth.
Never more than 48 degrees from the Sun along the ecliptic. She has a dense
atmosphere of carbon dioxide and suffers a dramatic greenhouse effect with
temperatures pushing 500 degrees Centigrade. Sulphuric acid clouds obscure
Venus from direct view so that her surface is invisible except by means of radar.
There is a radar map of her surface produced by Magellan in 1990. '*Oudeis emon
peplon aneile.*' What I get from today is that I am a pond. So often all we see are
the plants, the reeds, creatures that land in the water, waves. But this is not me. I
am the pond. The I that looks cannot look at itself (it is like the Sun, the source of
light and seeing). Thou art mine, I am thine, of that must thou be sure. Thou art
locked in my heart. Lost is the little key. Within must thou always be.
He looks at his own soul through a telescope. What seemed all irregular he sees
and shews to be beautiful constellations. And he adds to the consciousness hidden
worlds within worlds. '*The light foot hears you and the brightness begins.*'

6. A Star in the Hollow of His Hand

She holds the planets and a third of the sky in the beak of her mind,
scorches the mountain with the dark inferno of her cornflower eyes,
rocks her speckle-backed chair,
ponders her mad son,
hears a falling star.

It bounces down the mountainside,
cupped in its crescent box,
clatters like an empty ice cream carton from the gods at the Coliseum,
scatters clouds of sparrows.
Every stone it touches hisses and sizzles,
one by one.

She tautens on her back the buckled sinews of purple-in-the-heat massifs,
erects on them Earth's flock of rising foam-white, fish-crazed gannets,
whirrs into the glitter,
the bee swarm,
the heather haze,
the black ness.

There,
in her hidden meadows,
below the heather,
the culprit kneels,
a star in the hollow of his hand.

7. Hazy All Over Titan

In the morning she put three newlaid eggs in a bag
which you nested in your fox-fur cap and later reported
eaten, all three, in an omelette, for a late, late
lunch. Then you turned and ran, your leo-
pard pelted frame sending back its pulses of energy.

As you gazed back at her body
under its glittering tent
hooked onto her eastern limb
where a yellow curve showed the cleavage
of day and night,

as you gazed back at your smog-enshrouded
lover's receding crescent about one day after closest
approach – the lover who lured you to look
in a mirror then killed you (was it you
you were looking at, was it you that she killed?) –

the slight bluish glow of her haze was licking
all along her limbs, at the last swallowed up
in your gaze, dismembered, boiled and roasted,
apart from your heart, from the first fly-by
of the 30,000 particularities,

when all she'd wanted to say
was how much she missed you and how very strange
it was to be apart. It was Pallas rescued the heart,
and by this action you sprang forth hazy
all over Titan again in your former glory,

you ran a kilometre race,
you lunched on two lemons and two avocados,
said 'These may be ripe
by the time you take
one long, last look.'

8. The Thread

Whoever you are with your moonsilver gossamer voice in the dark,
don't sing to me of the hawk,
don't sing to me of Jupiter, or Saturn,
or a coiled up golden fleece,
mysterious one.

Give me a ball of your thread to unravel in the maze,
as your dark form with its voice attached seems to hover somewhere overhead.
Give me Kepler's five solids
unbubbling from Mercury,
this near-solsticial day.

Harness my tangled skein,
unpick it, hold it, steer with it through the labyrinth,
for love, being an elaborate spiral
and, on the logic above, awaiting discovery in a maze,
a maze which is the path to the heart,
is, in passing, you.

Something happens at the intersection of our paths.
A stone nestles there,
as one day nestle spheres within spheres,
and as we have meaning in that which is greater.
We were returning home. Now we go within.
The circle is square.

And if it is dark, it will be light.
If Earth seems a circle, a circle in a dodecahedron, not a sphere,
even if I don't expect it, yet it will be so,
the discovery of the route out,
in a tiny letter within a letter within a letter within a letter,
in which you wrote: Gemini, Bull, Venus, the May, Communication.
I did not expect the Solar System.

Come to me now, invisible singer
of love. Direct
this expedition to the heart,
quiet singer of love in the heart,
as the Galactic intersects the Ecliptic.

Silence

I want your thorns,
hang my stick
in your crook.

Rose petals glisten
on the stones.

This Night

1. This Night

At dusk stars penetrate
dark hugenesses

above the hidden river path
white with blackthorn flowers

whose leaves uncircle
around their fivenesses.

Dense trees
joust in the shadows,

carry dark rooms,
develop likenesses.

Clouds, even the hugest, only mute
daylight, that toothed leaves come,

at night deflect stars and moon,
reflect earth light.

Except this night.
They hug their pregnancies.

Earth light is out. Black
thorn blooms lie on the ground.

2. We Left a House

Light from the house
behind us dissolved
in effervescence.
We crossed four bridges,
then clouds rolled over.

We left a house
to find a river.

Darkness distilled
to its quintessence.
With only a stick
and my two lieges,
I clutched at twigs.

We left the river
to find a star.

By feet and skin,
by the stump
of a broken chestnut tree
we found the fifth bridge
and crossed the river.

3. The Fifth Bridge

What is the sound of the rails, whose four
shadows line the shuddering concrete? Are they salt?
Do they smell of the sea? Do the animals see
their colour turquoise, feel the roughness of flaked
iron that runs their length across the river? Had I known
these things, would I have been lost where now the sun
prints martins' wings in the dust, and the paths
gobbled by the waters are thick with wild garlic,
meadowsweet, water avens, grasses, where crows
speculate in the tall trees, and rocks stand ready to fall
above the narrow meadows? Where the causeway
trickle shrinks day by day, where butterflies chase
in circles above the butterbur? Where the mutilated
willow buds, and bright ribs move across the water?
Where the duck with her young amongst the sun
white stones flies upstream? Where silence is thick with haw?

4. A Riddle

What is this hyalite

rising like a field of sparrows,
schrift in blood,
boned in green,

manifest as two white shadows
running in the darkness at my side?

5. Mass

We have come into a hidden world
where silence hums
an invisible mass,
a shadow

of suns,
a music
philosophers don't know,
a rippling halo,

holy hope,
provisional dark
of burning star
and satellite.

What is it to see
in bent light?
to touch
the hand that locks

mass and gravity,
extent
that in our visible matter hide –
the moistness

in the golden ring
the bridegroom did for none provide
but for his bride,
the paradox

upon this hill
I need no glass
but that desire should fill
me more, not less?

6. Dropping the Stick

Some things it takes a telescope to see,
others a microscope.
But the instrument to see
what has never touched
skin, ears, mouth, eyes, nose, or memory

is my lover's eyes.

This that I drop and lose,
illuminated,
glitterous as dancing shoes

between our eyes.

The Venus inside.
The seed of the planet.
The spell.
The thumb on the rosary bead.

The torsion
as each constellation
comes into attention.

7. How We Got Home

It was March, so it must have been spring,
but cold, and the river was high,
bubbling like wine,
which I saw with the eyes
of the one who was close to death at the time,
but persisted, and therefore
they persisted with me
in my studied, clumsy course
on what was, admittedly,
a narrow path.
No evidence was later found
of the spot, nearly four-fifths round,
we were forced to turn back.
No mark, no stick. We must have reached
a wordless core, for we turned in unison –
no need for the question *where are you?*
even on such pocked and dark terrain
and for such a length of time, time
being our language, as if the bridge
crossing provided all the compass or clock
we lacked, its structure an entrance,
its purpose defined by our unity, we three,
our common music which we carried
everywhere and asked with to cross
the first bridge again to the bank
which overlooks the Tyne and the Black Burn,
to turn there one last time . . .
       This was Jack's last walk.
On the night he died I walked there with Hawthorne
at dusk. At Martins' Dive a frantic tussling
took the weeds at the edge of the path. Was it perhaps
an injured rabbitling? No, this creature snapped
side to side and tunnelled the grass,
cleared the path and the mush, then plopped
in the water, breathed and began its seamless passing.

8. Bitumen

It tipped and clanged in the boot.
I stopped the car and righted
the dented snapple,
gingerly drove on.

When the man in the warehouse had seen
my attempt to lift the five gallon can
he stepped in,
turned it in his hands like an apple.

Tommy had noticed the barn
door, side and roof shedding black,
said 'They've not been done
this past forty year –
the place is going to rack and ruin.'

So barn and shed
are all to be darkened
with oil derivative,
extreme black unction spread
with a kitchen broom,
glossy, rich and thick, flammable, protective,
greedy for light.

Elegies

for Douglas

1. As the Clock Ticks

Every two hours throughout the night
as the clock ticks
a bell chinks.

Under the snuffed moon
the world sings.
He shoves the door,

admits
a crack of light
in which he stands

and looks.
The chain slung
round her neck

threads twin
enclipped
gold faces,

awaits the silent
slither of gravity,
her awakening,

the sun,
the dark interior
of the earth.

2. He'd Been Up In the Night

A man crouches in a tree,
over a stream in twilight

his red tartan scarf stretched
out across the hallway

his stick and bundle on the shore,
his dog behind him

stools and chairs were askew

and in the foreground
water creatures surface,
beavers, otters, looking at him

Christmas knicknacks lay
on the floor, spilt
from a reindeer's carriage,
coals tumbled on the hearth

his head points down,
he watches for something
in the water

books were pushed back
on the table, *The Screwtape*
Letters uppermost.

The tree bears his weight.
It bears the weight of the world.

3. The Three Bearing Gifts

The three bearing gifts arrive.
A white bath plank, a frame
with a funnel for the toilet, a piece
of tubular steel to bolt
to the bed. A wooden cross
with rubber battens to lift
the chair. One of the three
explains to the others where
things go and how they work.
Then they call you. You rise
with difficulty, like a wet butterfly
on its first flight and no legs
to speak of. I forcibly hold
my hands behind me, try not
to help. They make you cross
a hand over to hold a rail.
Awkward. You turn. Left
and right and back and front –
all one to you. Later
that night I come to see you.
You lie flat, eyes blank as slivers
of snot. I kiss your dry
forehead. You raise your hands
to touch mine, smile, kiss
me back. 'I saw a fish come in,'
you say, 'and it said it was going
to the fridge.' Five days later
the three return with a gleaming
Zimmer frame. 'I'm not
getting up,' you say. You want
a drink. 'Something oily.'
So I give you the energy drink
and you tip the whisky in it.

I ask for your teeth. You hook
them out of your mouth and into
the whisky glass, trail glistening
strings of mucus and saliva.
'How do you feel?' I ask.
You say 'I'm better today,'
latch onto my hand in the warm,
twitchy depths of the bed.

4. Except the Trees

Inside magnolia walls,
on a bed huge as the Constable –
a cart at a dusty waterhole
in a distant summer –
you are looking up into a deep
space, parted lips slack
to the curve of a dolphin leaping
on indigo foam, a whippy
tartan fleece. In your sleep
you flatten your knees
on the floral sheet. You push
them up and down in waves.
Your curling fingers claw
the top of the quilt. A glass
of water stands cold and clear
on the cabinet. A teddy bear
plies you a padded heart. A pair
of slippers loaf on the floor.
Curtains swag the view. A glimpse
of shimmering nimbus,
blind in the sun, unrolls
on turquoise. Everything
is – the rug, grass-damp, the pair
of specs set free from its case,
bitten sweets, skewed biscuit
tins on the window ledge, squeezed
tubes, the pack of wipes, the pads.
And outside, everything holds
its icy whiteness except the trees,
whose branches dip, release
their powder, rise.

5. The Birth

The pregnancy passed almost without incident.
The nausea in the first few months. The blood spotting.
The scans, the visits to the local infirmary, with doctors'
visits between. The weighings. The takings of blood
pressure. The groups of people gathered round,
clucking breathe like this, hold on to that, eat the other,
telling stories of horror, hours of agony. The three
bearing gifts, the frame, the rail, the chair,
the toilet on stilts, the three months supply of nappies.
Then the day arrived. We hadn't expected it.
You were unusually talkative. Plump and translucent
as basalt on your pillows. You breathed a little sharply,
then stopped, and as the nurses wrapped your face
in white and stamped your nose, the curled thing rose,
bloody and pink, from where I'd massaged body oil
in the curve of your thighs six hours before, and split
the air with screams and pummelled me
till my breastbone cracked. I laid it
on the needle quivering still in your side,
squeezed the milk from its mouth into your veins
in the usual way before I said goodbye.

6. I Have Left the Glass of Water

I have left the glass of water –
so cold and clear –
on the coffee table
by the fireside.

Your chair waits
for you to come and squeeze
it and lift the glass, tilt
it to your lips.

You left it half full
on the day
they took you to the hospital,
hooked you to a drip.

The day after,
a dry tissue lay where
you'd scrunched it,
between your tobacco and your pipes.

7. The Plum Tree Has Split

Last year there was a glut of plums.
They ripened and fell on the cracked glass panes.
I rescued as many as I could. I washed the ones
that glowed orange and gave you those that were whole.
You took a bite, sucked and spat out the rest.
You threw the half-eaten sugary lumps on the fire and missed.
I picked them out of the soot.

This year the plum tree has split
right through to its orange heart.
It is bent with the weight
of green fruit clustered in tight
bunches. Will there be water
enough through the torn tree's xylem
for exiled fruit to ripen?

We shall see,
by the difference between
the torn-off fruit
and the rest of the tree.

8. Boxes

A man came in a van with three huge boxes I had to sign for. Under the cardboard flaps were glistening plastic packs of incontinence pads. I stowed them mostly in the roof where they still are, insulating the roof as what would have been your 93rd October 5th approaches. There are three boxes of Swan Vesta matches next to the pots of pipes and pipe parts by your armchair next to the fire and I noticed that two have a little corner missing where you tore it between your thumb and finger to get more easily at the matches. One has a whole strip missing. Now there are four, since I fetched one that was deep in the glove compartment of the old car in which I brought you home the week before you died. Four shapes. Five boxes. A large box on the bottom, white inner drawer pushed slightly in. Dirty price tag visible, black print visible under perpendicular sandface of middle box, red, yellow, green lines visible under perpendicular yellow block ends not pushed in, one on the right with slightly sagging upper sleeve so sliver of black appears under the lightness of the top layer under the pair of swans, the box of red, the green, the white lettering, the shadow on the pink flowers on the paper on the plaster on the wall which bears plaster and paper and flowers and drops of your spilt blood in vertical streaks, knowing inside each box the strip torn out between your finger and thumb, three corners leaving soft nap, one amputated strip jagged, and in the bottom box two compartments, gun-metal dust, pink tips laid three to one and one to one on three white ends, the other compartments crammed with pink ends, two single cigar halves snapped in two but attached by a paper hinge, not severed.

9. The Black Hen Is Clucking

The black hen is clucking.
One of the eggs rolled loose,
covered in feathers and goo.
I took it to the shed.
It rattled, it.
She is clucking.
She is always there.
OK girl, I'll let you be.

The black hen has left her nest.
There are no eggs there,
only the crock egg.
She ranges the field
with the cock,
the other hen.
Neither of them
is laying.

10. Silly Hall

Here in the silence
above the black water,
the flecking foam,
the sandy mint,

most days I walk
to Silly Hall
and peer inside.
Once I heard the crack

of the hammer,
once saw movement
in the shadow
cool in summer.

I did not stay,
turned back through the wrought
iron gate, on the deer tracks,
brimming causeway,

parting high thistles,
over the bridge
to Bleagate –
Scarberry Hill –

where in the breath
before the wind
trees stand in silence.
Under the trees

there is always the hidden
and the more hidden,
there is always water
rushing towards water.

11. The Key

I thought we would walk there many times,
but this was the first and last,
in spring, soon to be summer,

to the highest bridge,
unbearable poise
where rests infinite weight,

against the pull
of the black centre,
larger than the sky,

in the silence,
with sound of sucked sap
and skylarks,

the start of a final journey,
in the stillness
when the wind pauses,

the moment between water and rocks,
between rise and fall,
at the point of no weight.

The shadows of the birds' wings
fell across the room
again and again –

a room we left for the ghylls
where water foams,
and wood sorrel and wild raspberries grow,

where different waters,
their many parts,
move as one,

in longitudinal, mechanical waves,
with banners and clocks,
by hand –

at this particular moment,
the hand on the latch,
the key,

the ninety-six birds
that cross the river in a boat too small,
by dint of attention.

We passed through the shadowed hall,
under the wooden lintel,
over the stile

to the place of the heron –
the fields of intuition
left unsown,

where three puffs of white smoke,
as the world wind paused,
were as bright an icon,

before it entered the air
held above and below,
as the rain of ocean.

12. Darkness

It was dark when I got home
to Scarberry Hill from Dove Cottage,
over the mountain. I left the door open.
The steps came in, the wooden rail,
the thoughts of the dead,
the mushrooms, the paeonies,
the thick night under pine needles,
the rosebay willowherb not yet in flower,
the sinking air, the dry-stone wall,
the flowering cherry, the water
skimming the underground pipe,
the cow shapes, the corner
of the bottom field, where
the lost geese folded their wings until
they were caught, the beach
at Brighton, the rain, the clouds,
the shifting, sucking, crunching
shingle, the eclipse of an uncanny moon,
the sea, the grey tufts topped
with the bobbing blackcurrants,
whipped turquoise salt-heave, the flattest
part of the world, the briar rose,
the shepherds' crooks hooked onto the door,
the biggest sky, the long descending road
to the Pitlochry salmon hatchery,
the rocky Highland roads, the MacCaig
tower, the view of the whole of Oban city,
the dog in his kennel, the stream,
Fort William with its one-way streets
and map shops, floating lambs'
tails, Chinese cafés and road
humps, the ferry to see the seals,
the single wooden seagull bobbing
up and down on a string in the hold,
the telegraph pole, the Christmas trees,
and the house at the top of the hill,
and the walk to the top of the hill
to see the lights still on.

13. Breath

Buttock chair top. Pigeon gap stone. Bird
feeder empty. Lungs empty slowly. Then
comes a moment they are filling again.
Raw, inside out, flying free. Tepid
and weak. Grey slits rainbow the pane.
Your skin, smooth, flaked, stroked. You
touched nape of neck to my front,
your skin to my heart. Breath, where
is breath now? Where did it stop? Did
it stop? Did it pass? What passes
by as light pushes the shadows
slowly under the trees
on this midsummer day?

14. Who Is the Salmon?

The water level was high even four days
after torrential rain, and yet not so high
that the river bed was invisible. The bracken had turned
orange. Under the trees by the river's edge
the water's surface shook, as if some creature
had eased itself out of the dipping branches
and slithered into the water. Further upriver,
an urgent splashing and commotion
in the water under a tree again announced
the entry of something from the air above. Or was it
something in the water rising to the surface?
Then, at a point where the water skimmed a flat stone
before it churned into a froth of foam at its base
there was a smack, like a wet sheet snapped to strip
it of water drops. Was it a salmon? A single salmon
making her progress upriver? Or were three
separate salmon choosing the same evening
with a favourable depth of water to swim
upstream to whatever the winter could offer of shelter,
sustenance and a haven for spawn? The next day
the water level was down. The sun shone right through
to the stones on the bottom. There were no salmon.

Might there be a point near the river's source
where the silver flash no longer needs
a covering of water or the time
between splashes but manifests without
the mantle of depth or trees or sky?
Did the sun shining have anything to do
with the shyness of the salmon on the second day
of observation? Or was it simply
a matter of leaves, that there were more,
shuttling each other on the surface,
one or two dipping to the bottom
like coins? Whoever it was belonged
in the world under the water's surface,
and not in this world between the water
and the outer surface of the atmosphere.

And above the welkin, who is it watching to see the splash in the air's surface, the movement, the disturbance? Who is it watching me write this now? Am I at this moment observing myself break out of some medium as real as water?

15. Night

Your stars begin to sizzle in the water.
Tall and dark as the sky, you wait
high over the river where day still itches
and sheep jiggle on the wooded hill,
unscattered by the streak of a dog.
As we walk to the broken old bridge,
an owl hoots over and over.
The river, the mist, burn silver.
I bend down. Night looks over my shoulder.
In the last harebells' hooded blue
you show me raging tempests,
buckling worlds of gas, bubbling gusts
of hot green hydrogen, red sulphur, blue oxygen,
torrents of ultraviolet smelting spheres within
the squeezed red hips, the blackened, pecked,
eviscerated hips, dangling their rags,
spilling seed, and the ripening sloes,
the phosphorescent grass, the dessicated docks.
The sun's rays bounce off the Pole ice,
a female at the end of her tether with no chance
against a Night Creature – a bear, a swan
or a scorpion. In starlight caracal catches spring hare.
Do your stars eat meat? If so, do they kill in silence
to avoid attracting the lions? lions who never roar
in the daylight. Caracal protects its kill from the aardvark
who in turn eats ants and termites, three hundred thousand
in a single night. Do they feed their young on starlight?
– the patterns on the water, overlapping circles,
expanding distant worlds invisible by day,
Sun's shroud of nearness. I no longer see the night
nor the illusion of Devil's Bit Scabious' spikes of blue
turned to fluff in the season.

16. I Am Not Sure to Whom I Am Speaking

I am not sure to whom I am speaking.
I am not sure who it is rumbling in my stomach.
I am not sure why laughter is bursting out of me
as well as tears.

Rain snivelled the windscreen,
the cobbles were shiny and slippy.
Mary the minister brought a cup of black coffee,
a surplice-white biscuit.

Then, from some cassock-black corner
appeared what I thought was a thermos flask
at first. Why is she bringing me
a thermos flask?

It looked heavy.
'Hazel the undertaker cares about you.
Hazel is a widow too.
Hazel understands.'

I lifted the maroon six-sided container,
like a pillar of whinsill in its cardboard
box, with an envelope sellotaped on,
and it was indeed heavy.

I walked down the street
on the hard slippy cobbles
with a hand on top as if to steady it,
walking behind it

as I used to walk behind you,
looking at you, directing my gaze on you.
I put it in the back of the car on the floor,
next to my bag.

At home Jack stood by his kennel,
Hawthorne sat on the wall. The door
swung open of its own accord.
I placed you in the window

next to the dry lily petals, their stamens still attached
and shedding pollen, next to the witch's hat,
the razor shells, the mermaid's purse,
and put on Pärt's *Magnificat*.

17. Dust

A dipper dropped out of the water
at its fastest moving point,
under the bridge, water
quite clear, yet burnished,
both showing and concealing
stones packed
in on the bottom.

A cloud of grit and dust
billowed in the air above the rapids,
then water closed over it,
tearing its fronds.

A few shakes and taps
sent the last puffs
onto languorous silks
curling at the edge.

A rinse in an enclosed pool
left the urn bright
with standing water drops.

Cracks in the rocks at the centre
held the white crumblings
as water moved over
them tugging fragments away,
one or two at a time.

Water ribs around the stones,
all moving at different speeds,
in different directions,
at different rolling angles,
added their sounds and movements
together into a single
grandeur of turbulence.

Next day some lines of sandy
grit lingered in grooves
under the spreading sheets
of water. A few grains spilt
on the bridge remained.

But the day after that, rains
and swollen river had washed
all away in a great sigh
into green, opaque depths.

The rising torrent had even the grooved
rocks embraced
in its intelligence.

18. Interior Life

After three years have passed I open the bag,
keep the soft beige socks in the red stripe tartan,
wash and keep the folded white singlet vest,
wash the folded blue short-sleeved thermal vest,
keep the Calvin Klein red tartan underpants,
bin the wrinkled pale-blue braces,
wash the red tartan pyjama top,
cut off the buttons and burn the blue pyjama bottoms,
pull on and wear the maroon cashmere V-neck sweater,
wash the blue Racing Green shirt,
wash one white hankie printed in lipstick pink,
give to charity the green cord trousers with buttons for braces,
to charity the dark brown cords with blue braces still attached,
to charity the cosy grey fleece,
to charity the navy-blue-to-black empty space at the bottom.

*

Today the water is low,
the stone divided in three.
The top is green,
there is a wet band
where the water had risen,
and a part still hidden,
enwrapped in its flow.

Thus the corkscrew insulted the bone-handled knife.
But the knife, with his multicoloured inlaid handle,
his flashing blade, was convinced of his own beauty,
and did not take to heart the insults. Instead,
he answered the corkscrew: 'Let me give you
a description of my Mother. My Mother is bright
as the sun and swift as a deer on the hill.
She is beautiful as the finest adornment of princes,
dripping with jewels. She has the precision
of a cylindrical nir stone seal. She circles with gold
the wrists and fingers. She is a living alabaster statue,
a protective goddess, on a turquoise pedestal.'

*

'I am the Truth.' Hallaj

The three swallows
one by one
darken the kitchen,
circle together
in the middle space
for some moments
then fly out through the door.

He was alone and sleep overcame him
in a flood, sleep that knows no master,
but is overpowering. On his bed
of linen and wool he lay down,
not to sleep, but to dream.
He did not turn back at the door
of the dream, for it tells the truth
to the truthful. It bellows like a bull.

*

A willow twig with young leaves
attaches itself to my neck
as I walk by the river.
I press it in the leaves
of my notebook.
Later its fresh green smell
sweetens the air of my bedroom.

It is a temple lofty and fearsome
in radiance. It is open wide.
It awakens the awesome.

The canals, levees and irrigation channels
are clear. Abundant water will never be lacking.

*

The boat enters the rolling water
on the shining river, the five-headed mace
at its bow. The boat bobs up and down
at the quay. It sails off into the reedbeds.
It strikes against the rising waves, stirs up
the encircling fish. The water sparkles luxuriantly,
as the twinkling of an eye, as the one day
of happiness in thirty-six thousand years
of silence. Having been given this,
life is sought for, the share of humankind.

Poems

Look, you say, turning your indigo eyes
around us to the four corners of the concrete garden –
there is a city behind me, another on my right,
and this last one is here on my left. But,
I ask, what are their names? You say them
once or twice, but refuse to repeat them
one more time when I fail to understand.

But you will read us poems.
The first is a bird which soars in the air
and performs an intricate manoeuvre.
The second is another bird. It flies in an arc
above us, from the space in front of you
up and over to the space on my left,
changing colour from red
to orange to blue. The third
is a sheet of paper you hold
in front of you, with luminescent
geometrical forms which merge
together, re-emerge, dissolve, re-form.

Then you press in my hands a bag
and depart. It is crammed
with sheets of paper, glossy,
ornate notebooks in every colour,
shape and size, and, under these,
two large sheets of laminated paper
inscribed with music.
And at the bottom,
in its own paper bag, a long
white loaf of soft and fragrant bread.

Invisible

Invisible, I hungered,
yet feared repleteness still.
My dryness was a desert.
I travelled to my fill.

Yet lack of fullness never hurt –
its shedding slowed, that's all,
as the snatching sirocco
moved in for the kill.

I was afraid of difference,
yet my only skill
was to mould it from the wetness –
an angel on the hill.

I wanted to hide my artefact,
yet it was there to see,
though I left nothing to detect,
beyond a smarting cheek.

If I had been a human –
only half a wind –
would I have found seclusion
and left the salt behind?

Visible

Out of sight but visible
to the very end,
I am the ancient parable
of the ones who stand,

of how I look into the day
and out of the night,
and hear a voice from darkness say
the world awaits its light.

I am the living and the dead,
original and new.
No matter what the story said,
each one is true.

My time will come, its final length –
infinity.
At its beginning, middle, end,
I am all three.

I make the days magnificent,
shining with night,
jezebelled with colours bent
out of stars' light.

Yet I will not protect you – mad,
sane or divine –
but that you watch to see me split
water from wine.

Had you the faintest lantern, brother,
I would be light –
either the one or its own other,
come out of night.

The Butterfly

Next morning I wondered where I'd gone wrong:
the speckled wine had stained the glasses
(words like heirlooms had filtered through)
overnight, sacred mushrooms
in their hierophantic power.

And it was still disposable,
that gigantic idea, like a flea cut out of
paper, but I put it by instead,
as if for a rainy day, as if
for a baby to solve as a jigsaw.

If I hadn't seen the path puddling
from the overflow next door or remembered
how a black shadow patting my head
once turned out to be a butterfly,
I'd have forgotten all the times when it didn't.

You

At the moment when you stop mid-step
and look into my eyes, as if at a ship
on the horizon, blue sea and sun, and light
drains out of the sky and your face is lit
by its own sun in the far-off land we will sail
to in the boat whose mooring line you are unwinding
slowly with your hand, free of all
its many twists and knots, untwining
till, untethered and tacking in stays,
the boat will float free off fenders, but for now
your hands caress the rope, and rays
of light in the harbour point to you and the shadow
of the watcher disappears and floods
the waxing moon in red Mars light behind the soft, deep clouds.

Eclipse

The steps were slippy with iced foam
under the froth of winter stars.

Earth's upper rim
was sucking down the full moon,
gorging on its white cusp-pair through painted lips,
chewing it to a flushed corona.

Between then
and the time I rose from bed
an hour or so later and eclipsed
with a coat my nakedness,

the dark maw nibbled
what was by the end
a shrivelled pink carcase,
then exited, left.

We missed the sight of the full regurgitated gobbet:
under its red light
we were drinking from the goblet
of each other,

your earth from my mandala,
my moon from your crescent,
my crescent in yours,
your fire, air, water in mine.

Can we get any closer
than earth and moon in the sky,
lipping the juices,
careful not to take too much of the mother
in our ecstasy?

In the Darkness

In the darkness I can see every line
of your face. As if you are in my womb.
Your fingers feel for its entrance and I
am your mother, imagining what you
will look like when you are born. When I climb
after you into the freshly laundered
white duvet, and look at your face as you
sink into an involuntary slumber,
tender are my feelings for you, as though
you were my child. I ask if you want
me to turn out the light, which I do, and
so we nestle into each other, my
back to your front, and suddenly you are
a grown man, and I experience all
the pathos of the intervening years
and attempt to quench your searching mouth by
placing on it my own though I must trust
and contort my body to reach it and
you are back inside me now and you are
feeling with your fingers the ripeness of
my nipples which you cannot reach with your
mouth yet as your body ripples inside
me and the filaments of your face take
shape and glow in that invisible space
and dizzyingly fill the space with light.

Spells of the Raven

Split a speel and I am there.
Lift a staen and I am there.

Who provides for the Hrafn his food?
Seavy Sike and Longtongue Beck.
Hungry heath and busy dod.

Yet shall I run in the russet squirrel,
above the ferns in the oaks and the mizzle.

Neither walking nor flying,
I'm gan hyem to the Eden.

Split a speel and I am there.
Lift a staen and I am there.

Who provides for the Hrafn his food?
Skelling Moor and Hrafnwic Fell.
Butter flosh and bedlam crag.

Yet shall I run in the birch white trout,
in the chalk clear burn and the kikkling rout.

Neither clothed nor bare,
I'm gan hyem to the Eden.

Split a speel and I am there.
Lift a staen and I am there.

Who provides for the Hrafn his food?
Flowering Wood and Jordan Hills.
Goodie feld and beggaram dun.

Yet shall I run in the kraking Hrafn,
counsel the soul of the resting hound swain.

Neither black nor white,
I'm gan hyem to the Eden.

Split a speel and I am there.
Lift a staen and I am there.

Who provides for the Hrafn his food?
Appleby Street and Kirkoswald.
Skinny brant and paradise clough.

Yet shall I run in the red scar berry.
Summer will come and the thorns gan merry.

Neither followed nor alone,
I'm gan hyem to the Eden.

Split a speel and I am there.
Lift a staen and I am there.